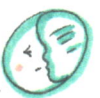

CameLoT

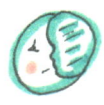

a Lot of CameLs

by Joann
Duff
Rosi

CAMELOT

a Lot of Camels

by Joann
    Duff
      Rosi

Christmas Eve 2013

It was a dark, cold, snowy night and the moon was just past full, shining brightly through the windows of the old house. I love to look at the moon, so, waking up I quietly tiptoed down the creaky steps to get a better view out the windows of the library. All of a sudden I heard a loud commotion followed by "arrumph."

Now I must tell you that when I was very young, my grandmother gave me a hand carved wooden camel that she had received from a missionary in Israel. Since then, for more than 50 years I have been receiving as gifts from parents, children, in-laws, friends and who knows who, camels - large camels; small camels, glass camels -

brass camels, tin camels, a
camel rocking horse, camel planters,
camel lamps, antique camels, stone
camels, you name it, I have it.
I guess when it is time for a
gift, a birthday, Christmas, Mother's
Day, a rainy day, a sunny day,
whatever, who would surmise, "Oh,
she loves camels."

    In any case, as I needed a place
to keep them, for them to live,
so to speak, on a shelf was placed
above the windows and books.
There they stay or stood, until
that night, or so I thought.

    I presume that you know
the ancient stories about animals
talking on Christmas Eve. I can
understand that for REAL animals
and understand that we humans
often do not hear them because we—

are all too noisy. But now I know that also UNREAL animals become REAL on Christmas Eve and they too can talk, and say more than "arrumph." The first who spoke was the first that I had received. Recognizing me he said, "HALLO! I have been waiting for you to come in on Christmas Eve. Say Hello to your Superiority."

"My what?" I asked. "Your Superiority; that is what a herd of camels is called. Because camels always think - or know - that they are Superior. Anyway, speaking for the entire herd, we are glad to see you and want to share our Stories."

My first camel told me that
he had heard the ancient stories
in Israel. Soon all of the other
camels began by telling me how
much they loved being in such
a large herd. Several repeated
that together they made a superiority.
They loved being together in my
library because, before they came,
many were alone, without another
camel in sight, noting that it
is hard to feel superior when
no one else is around.

Many commented on my
large collection of Christmas
books, several of which they had
read and enjoyed, especially those
about camels. Several said that
they had often laughed at the
many funny stories that I and my
family and friends had told around
the dinner table.

One camel, made of glass, while trying not to be too transparent, suggested that considering the superior nature of their "Superiority" that I should memorialize the evening with this book and that they would provide superior words of wisdom, in "Three Little Words." I agreed and here they are.

joannduffrose ♥

Edited by: Philys Rinaldo Rose ♥

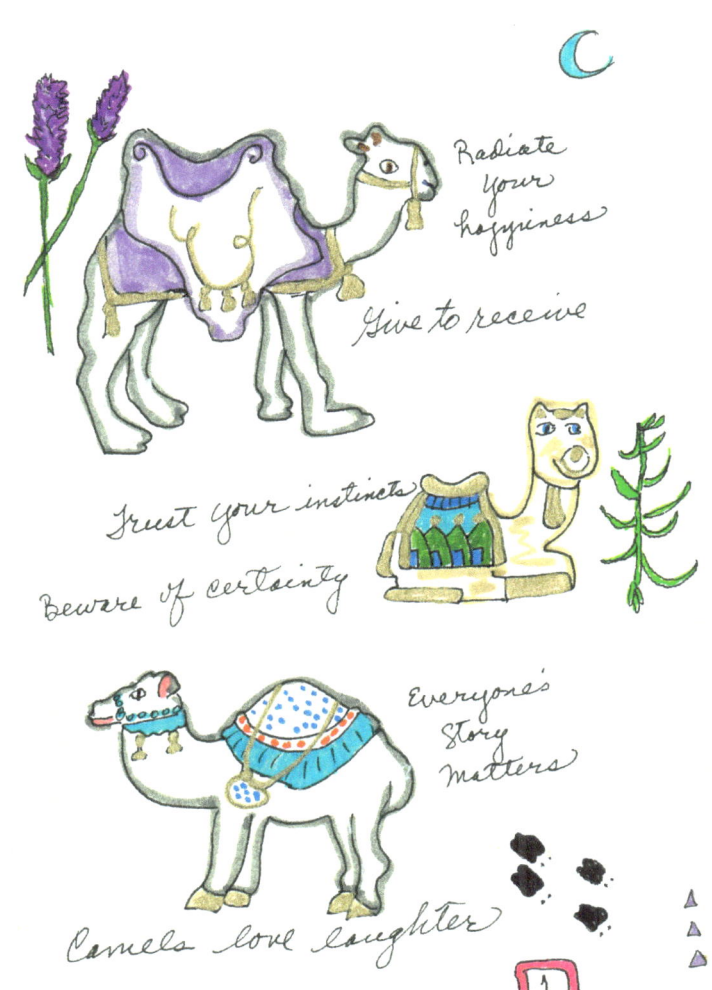

Radiate
your
happiness

Give to receive

Trust your instincts

Beware of certainty

Everyone's
Story
Matters

Camels love laughter

1.

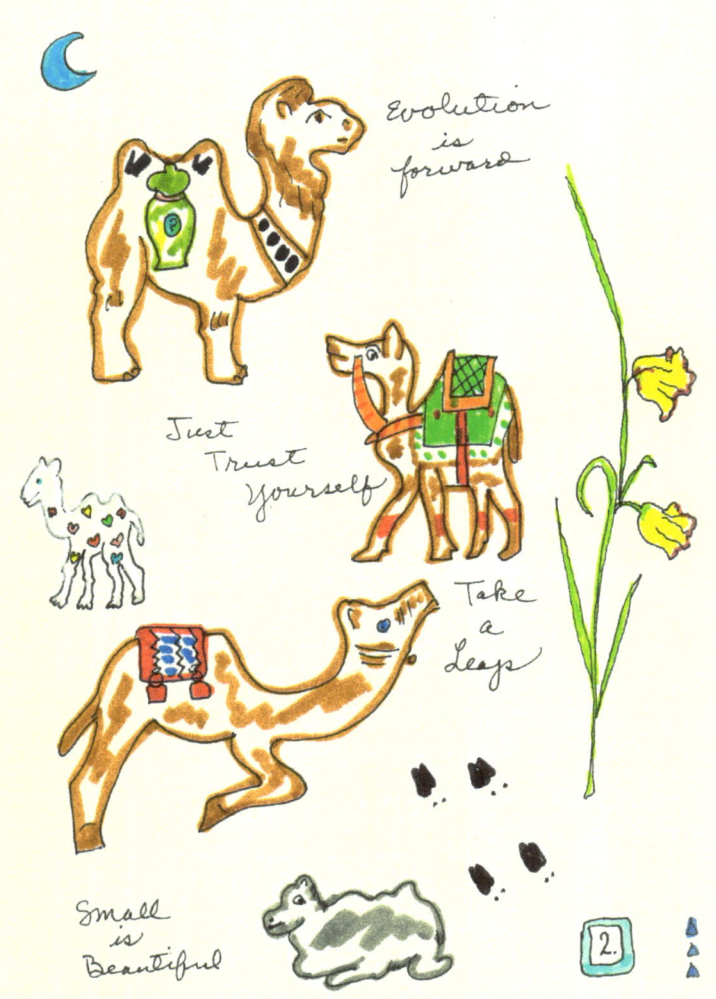

Evolution
is
forward

Just
Trust
Yourself

Take
a
Leap

Small
is
Beautiful

2.

Families
are Forever

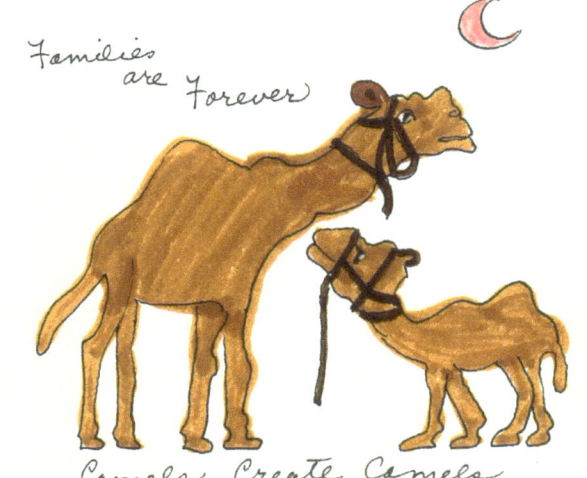

Camels Create Camels

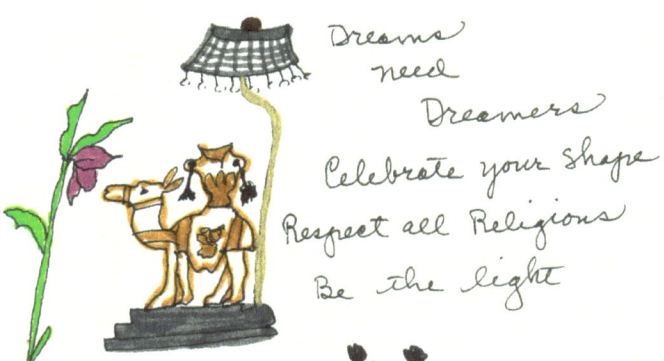

Dreams
need
Dreamers
Celebrate your Shape
Respect all Religions
Be the light

3.

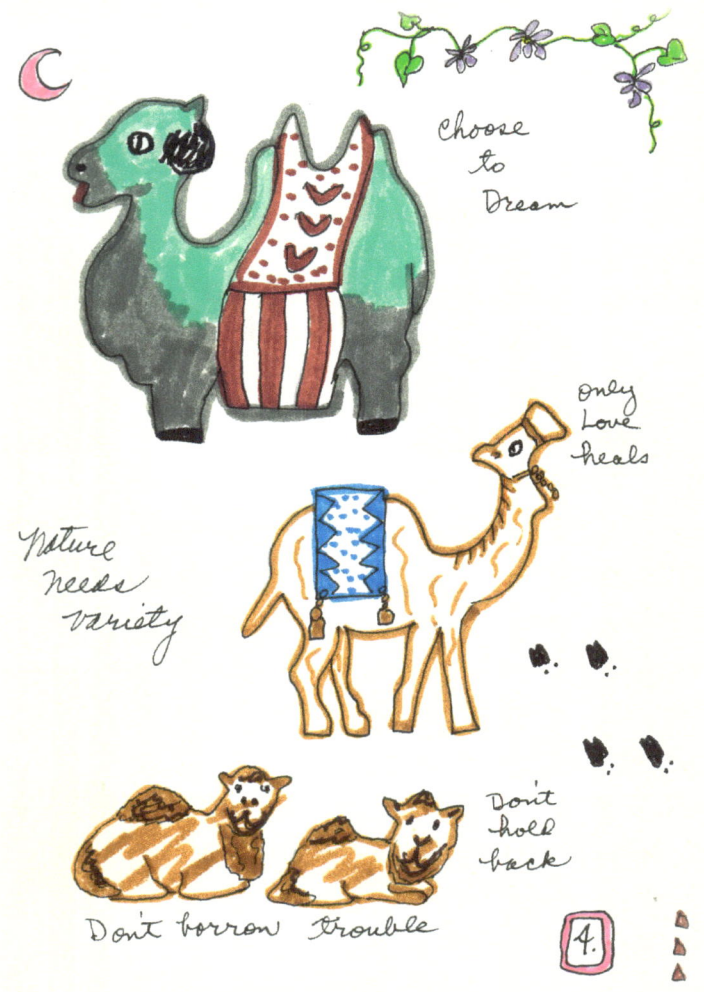

Choose
to
Dream

Only
Love
heals

Nature
needs
variety

Don't
hold
back

Don't borrow trouble

4.

Try being Cheerful

Find
Beauty
Everywhere

just
Be
Goofy

Remake your
Life

Give
Some
Warmth

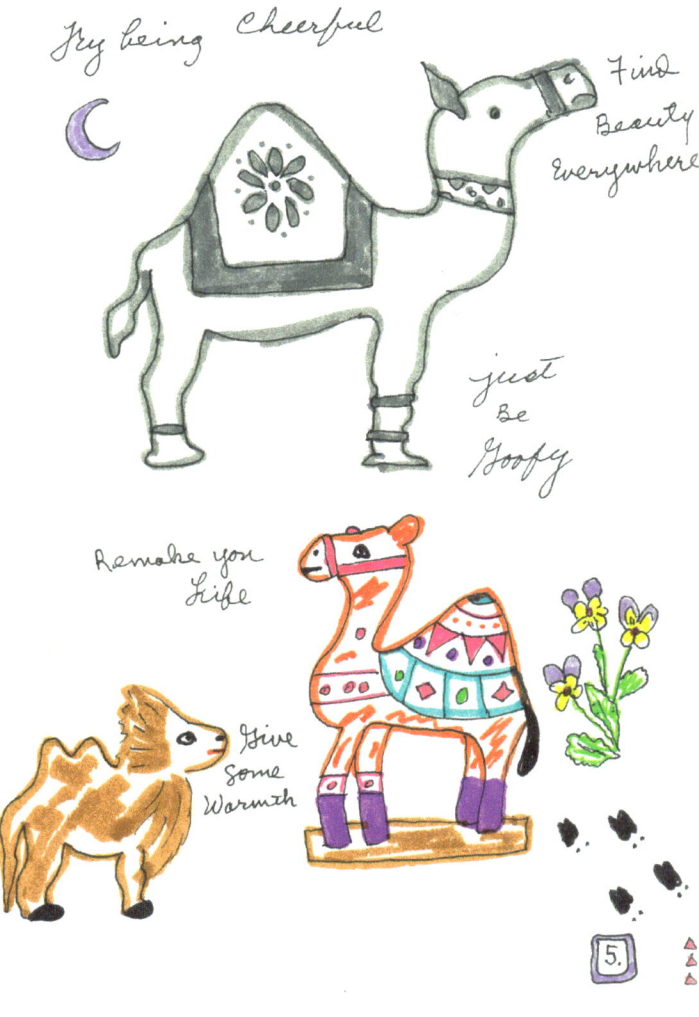

5.

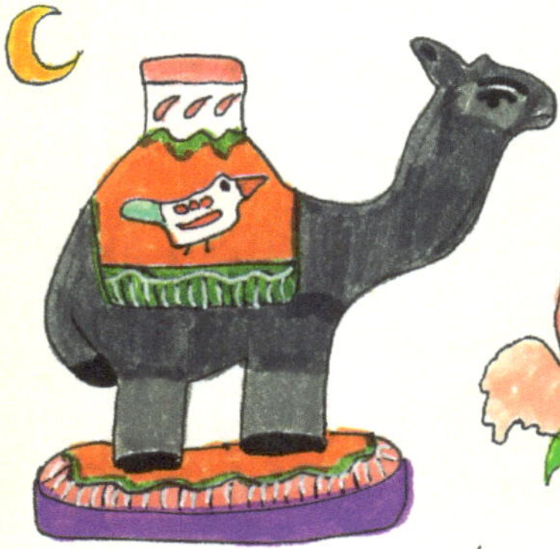

Love
the
Giver

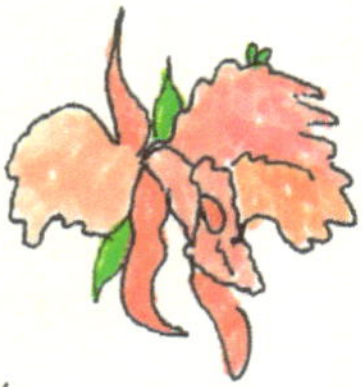

Invent new stories

Complaining
isn't
necessary

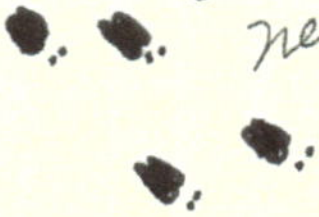

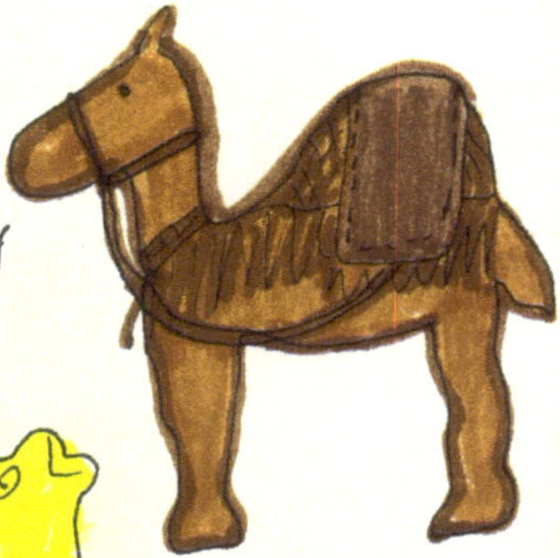

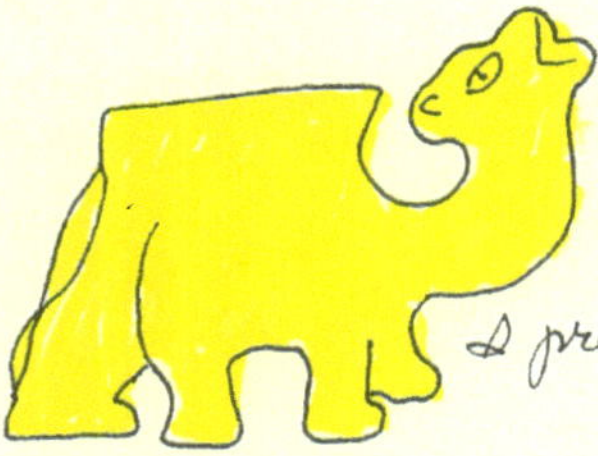

I prefer imperfection

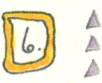

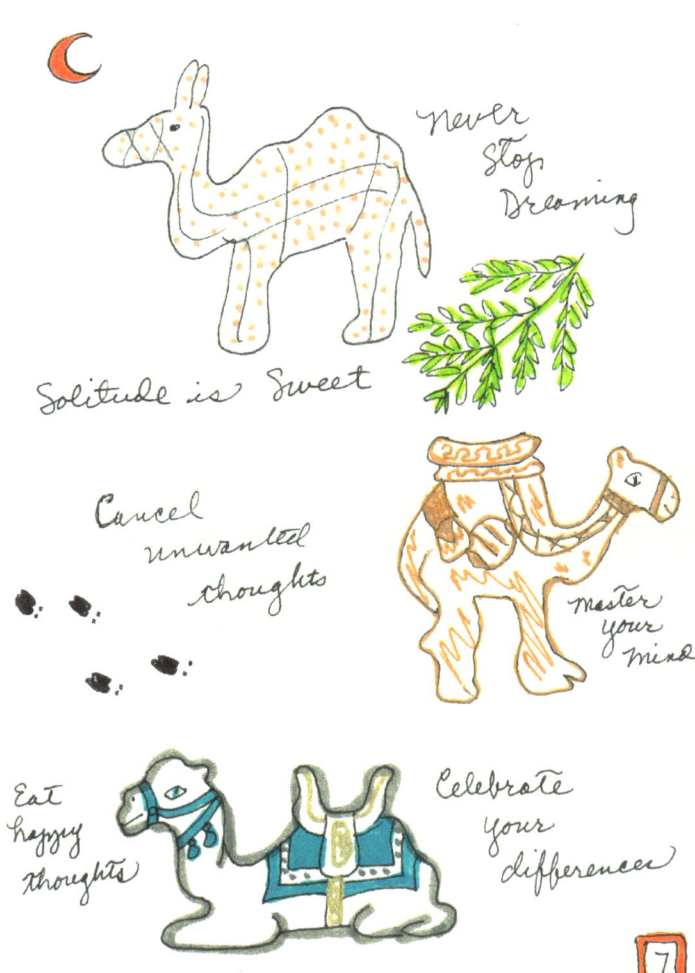

Never
Stop
Dreaming

Solitude is Sweet

Cancel
unwanted
thoughts

master
your
mind

Eat
happy
thoughts

Celebrate
your
differences

7.

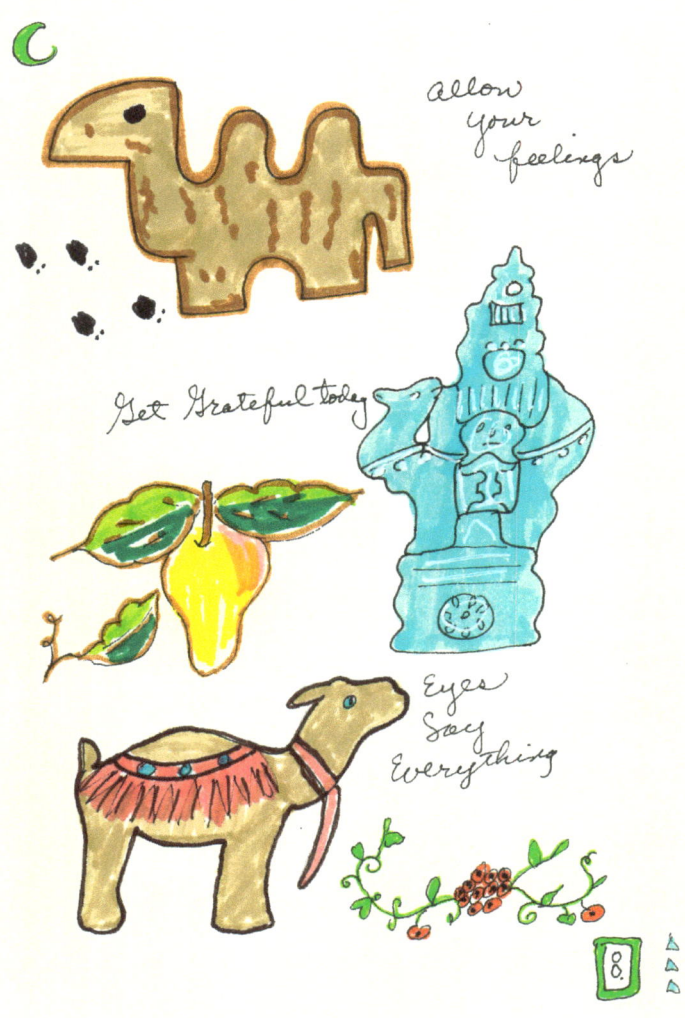

allow
your
feelings

Get Grateful today

Eyes
Say
Everything

Stand Up Shining

Just
Be
Brave

make
joyful
noises

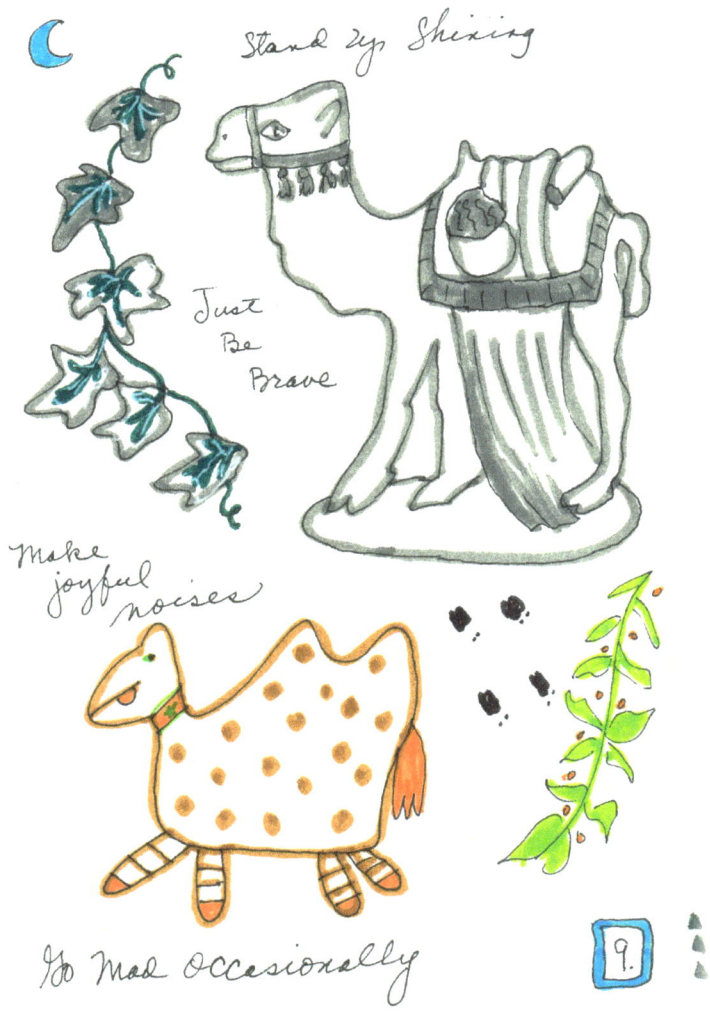

Go Mad Occasionally

9.

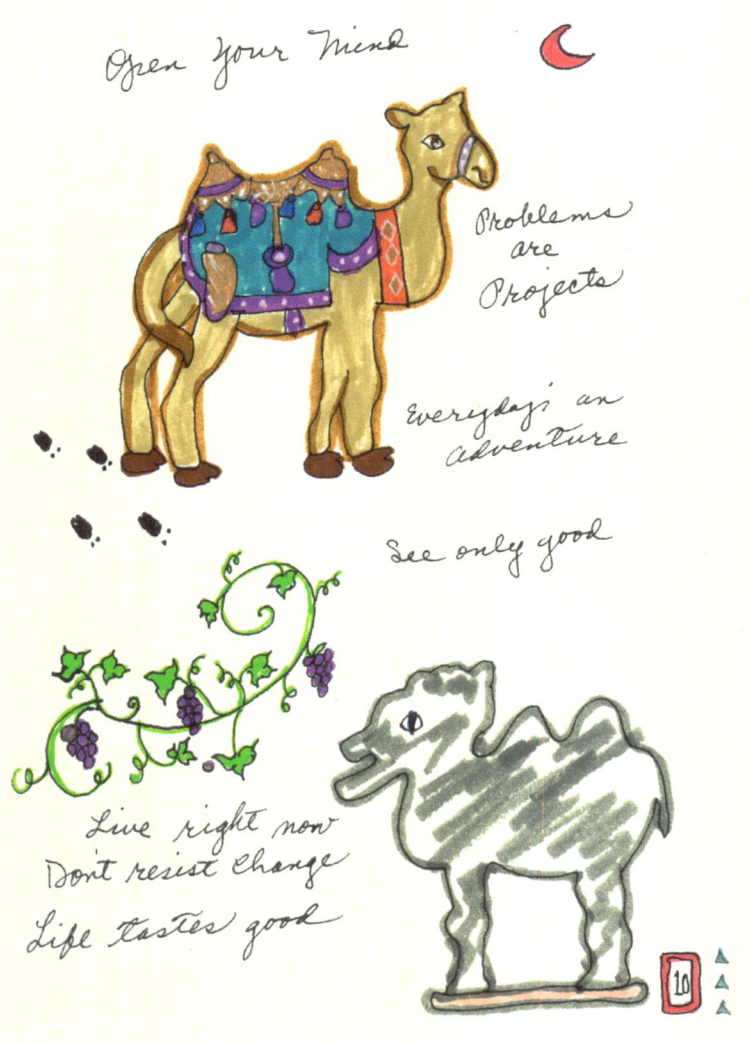

Open Your Mind

Problems
are
Projects

Everyday's an
adventure

See only good

Live right now
Don't resist change
Life tastes good

Reality is illusion
Establish new patterns
Love does wonders
Be the exception

Freedom's your Birthright

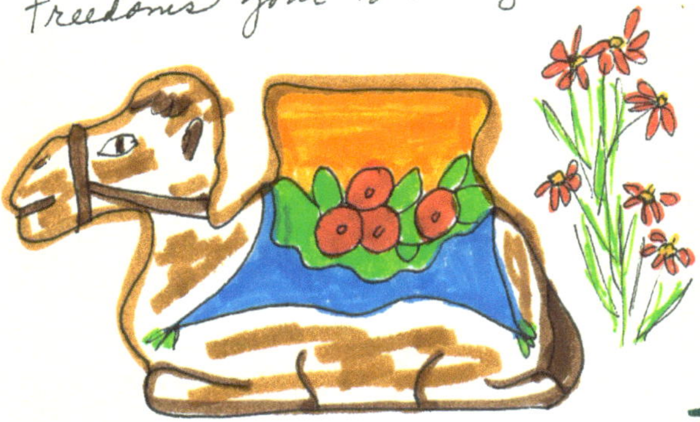

Create inner peace

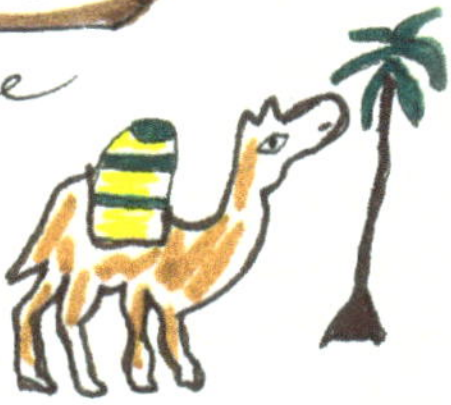

Give Thanks daily
Have more fun
Believe in Goodness
Courage is contagious
Choose to forgive

11.

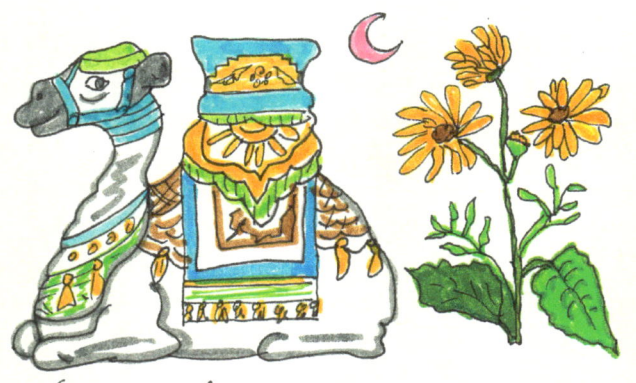

Welcome the unexpected
Astonish each other

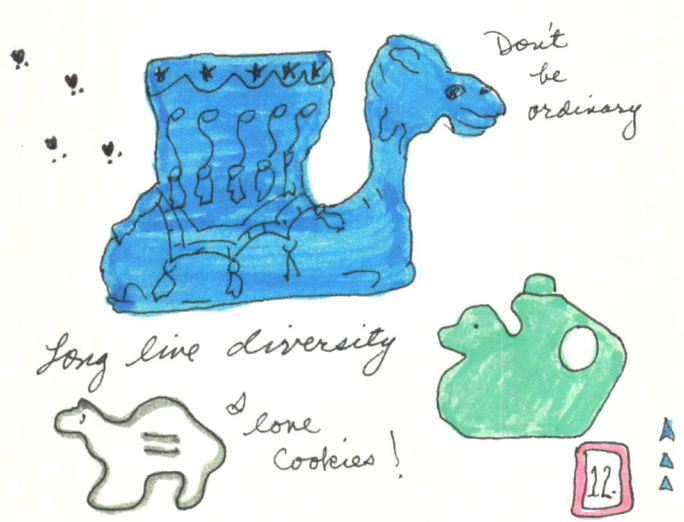

Don't
be
ordinary

Long live diversity

I love
Cookies!

12.

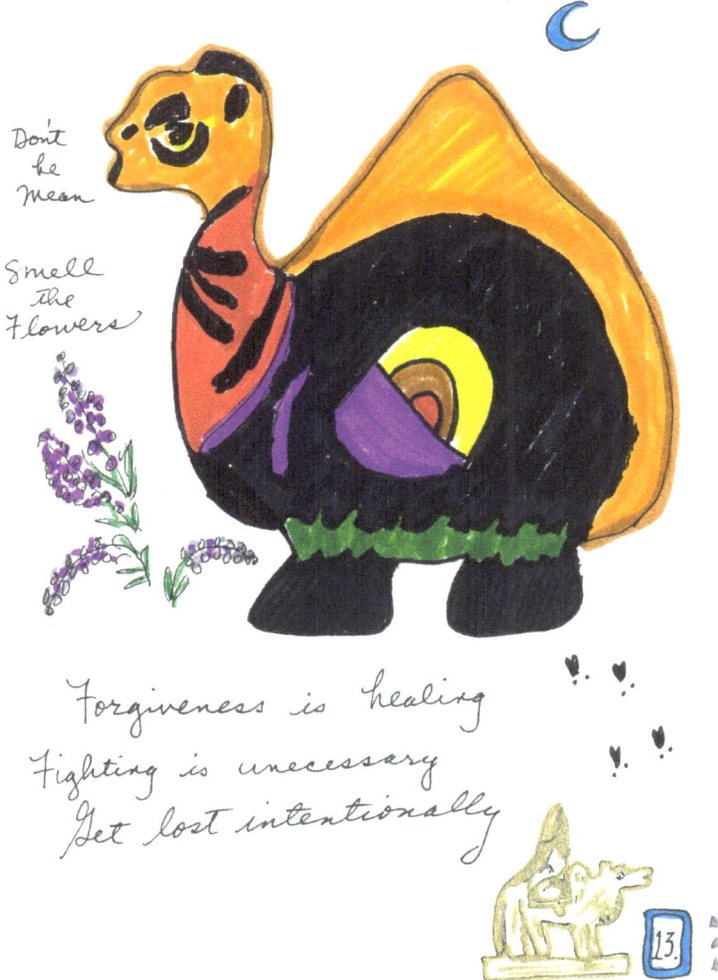

Don't
be
mean

Smell
the
Flowers

Forgiveness is healing
Fighting is unecessary
Get lost intentionally

13.

See
New
Worlds

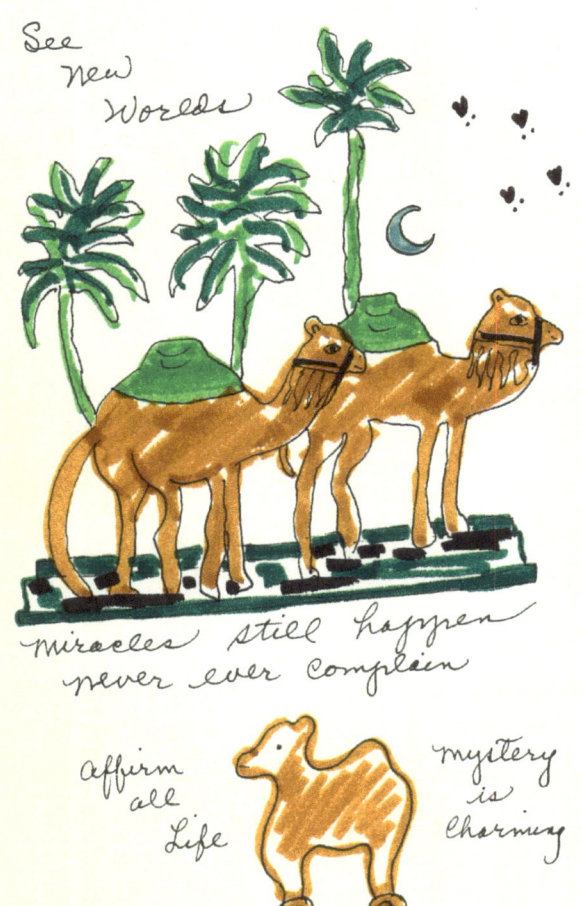

miracles still happen
never ever complain

affirm
all
Life

mystery
is
charming

14.

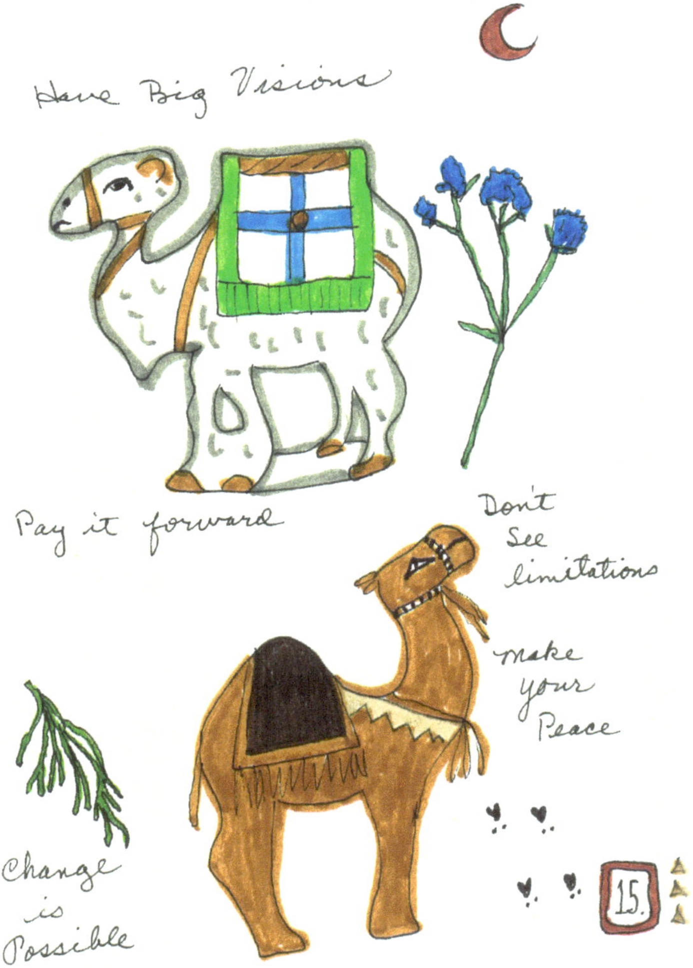

Have Big Visions

Pay it forward

Don't
See
limitations

make
your
Peace

Change
is
Possible

15.

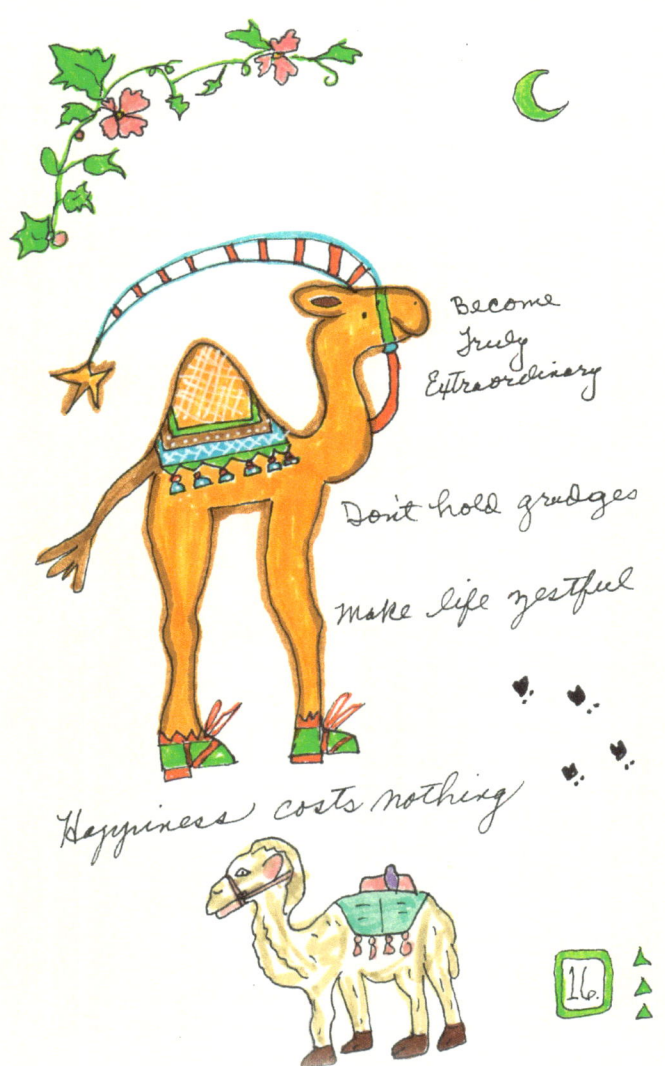

Become
Truly
Extraordinary

Don't hold grudges

make life zestful

Happiness costs nothing

26.

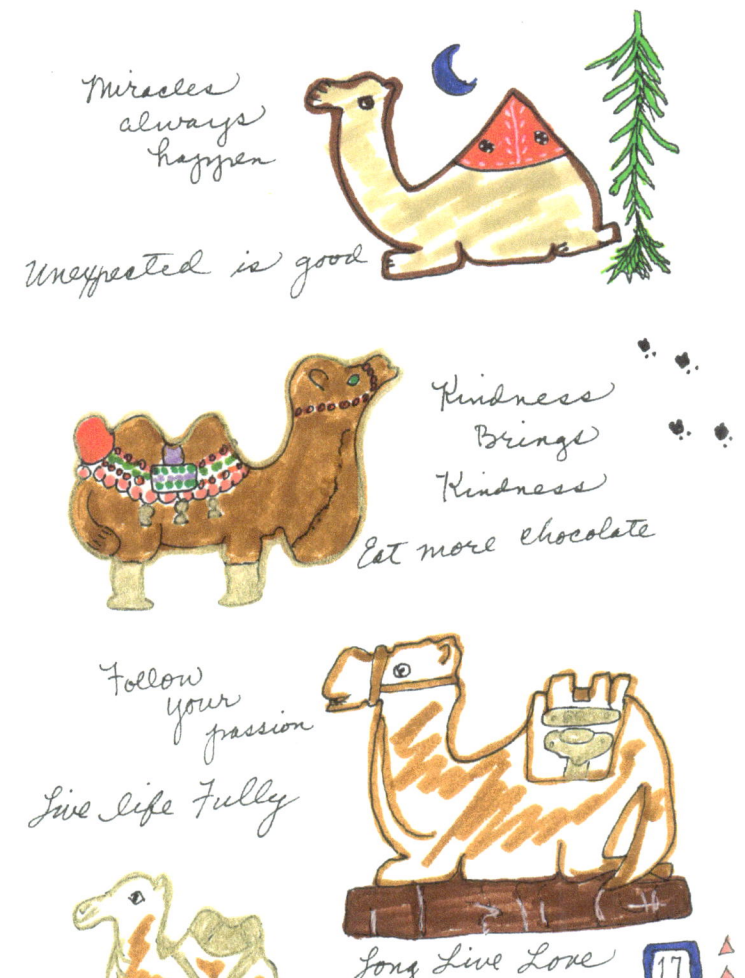

Miracles
always
happen

Unexpected is good

Kindness
Brings
Kindness

Eat more chocolate

Follow
your
passion

Live life Fully

Long Live Love

17.

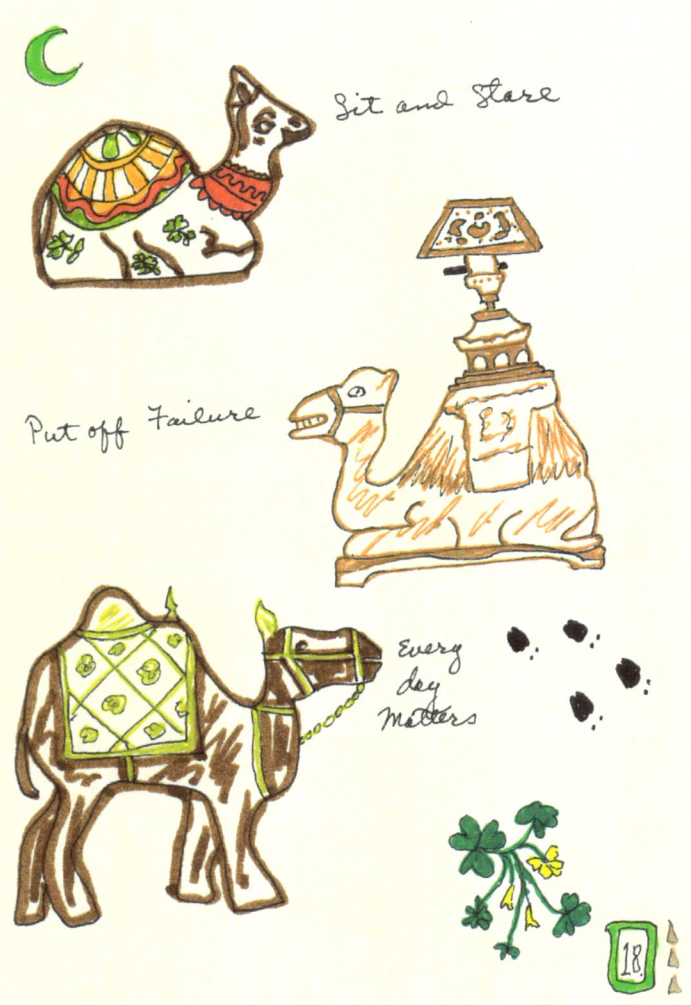

Sit and Stare

Put off Failure

Every day Matters

18

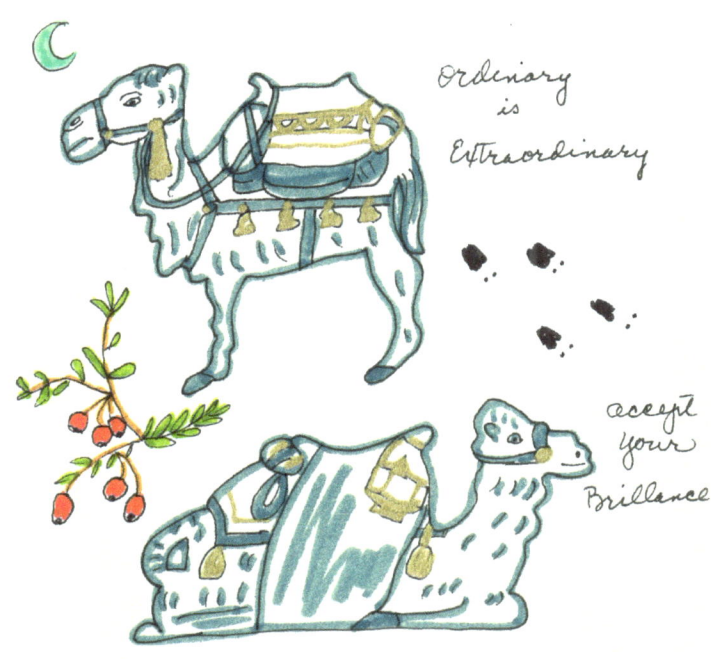

Ordinary
is
Extraordinary

accept
your
Brillance

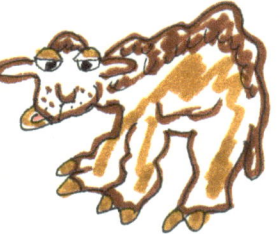

Imagine
and
Play

Pretty
doesn't
Matter

19.

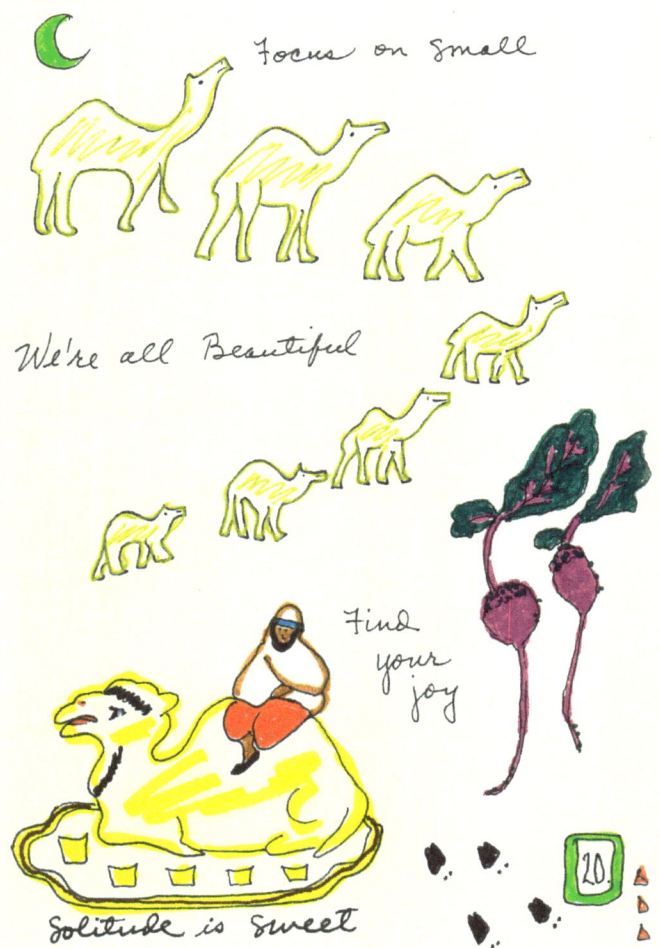

Focus on Small

We're all Beautiful

Find
your
joy

Solitude is Sweet

20.

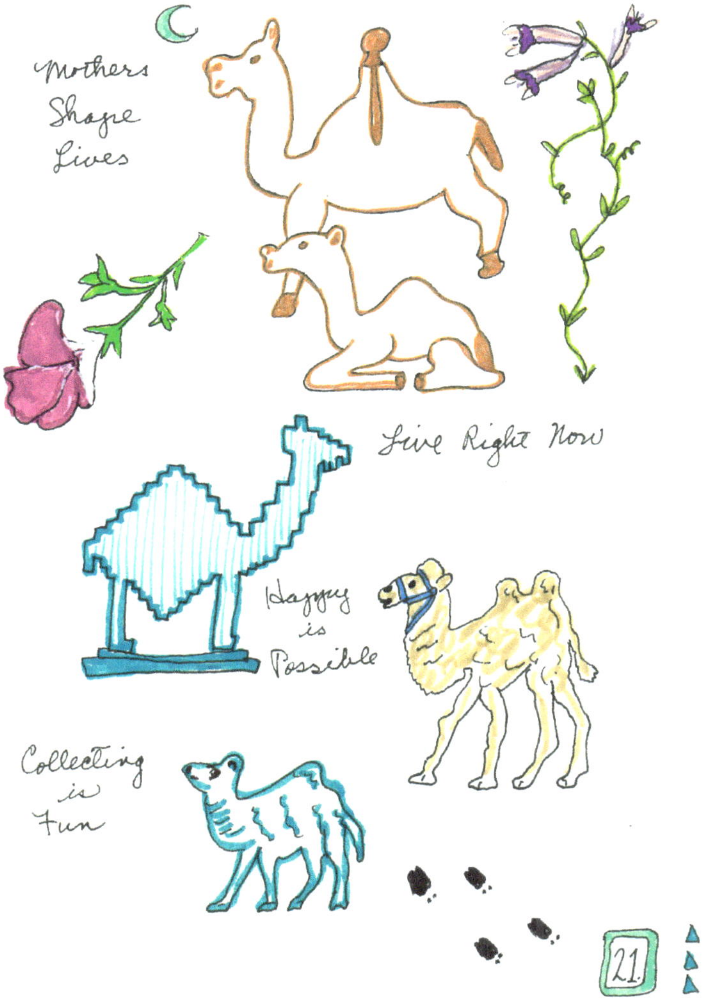

Mothers
Shape
Lives

Live Right Now

Happy
is
Possible

Collecting
is
Fun

21

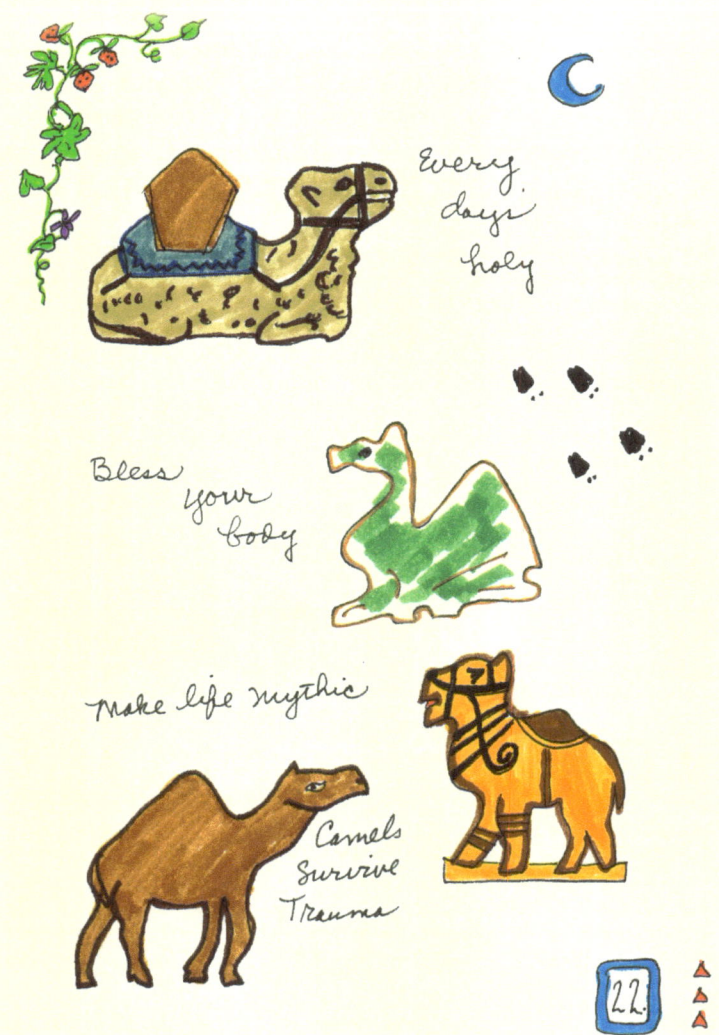

Every
day's
holy

Bless
your
body

Make life mythic

Camels
Survive
Trauma

22

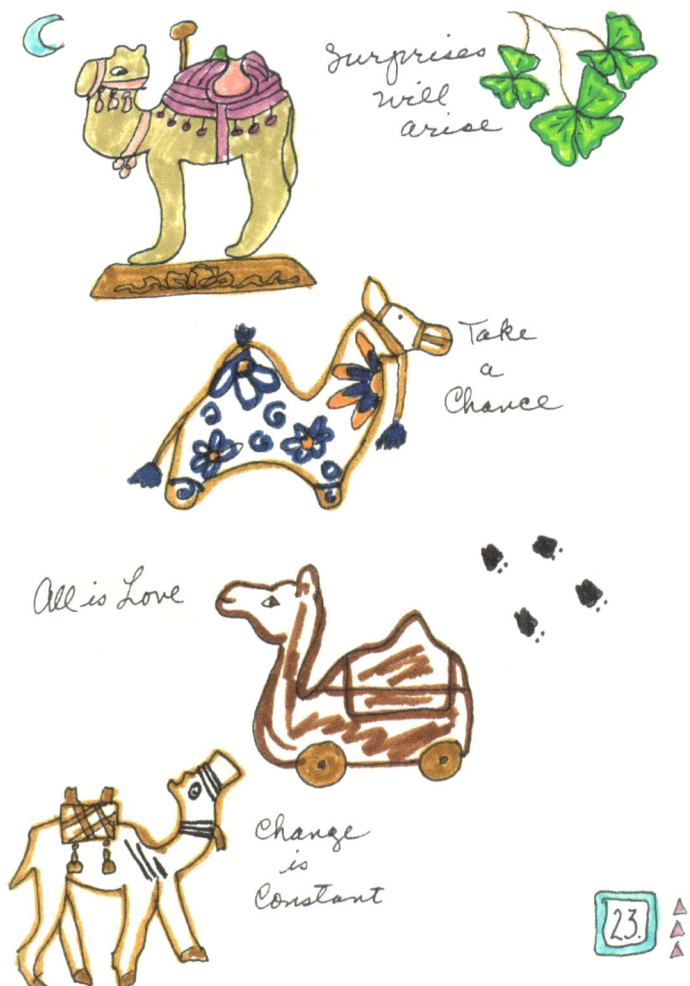

Surprises
will
arise

Take
a
Chance

All is Love

Change
is
Constant

23.

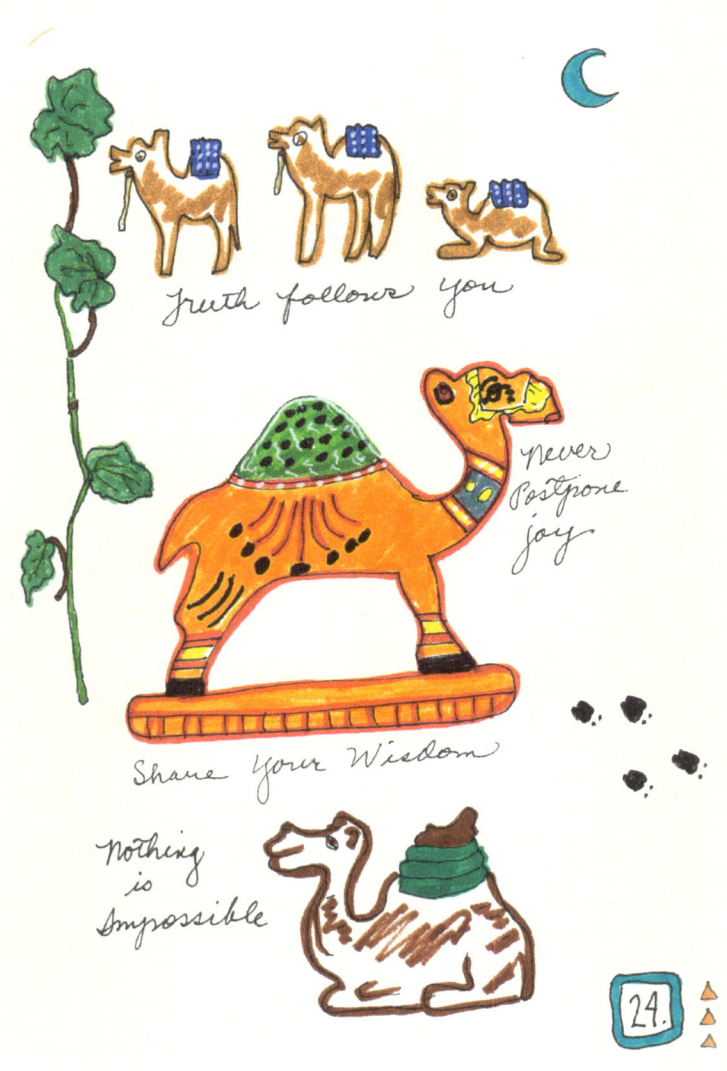

Truth follows you

Never
Postpone
joy

Share Your Wisdom

Nothing
is
Impossible

24.

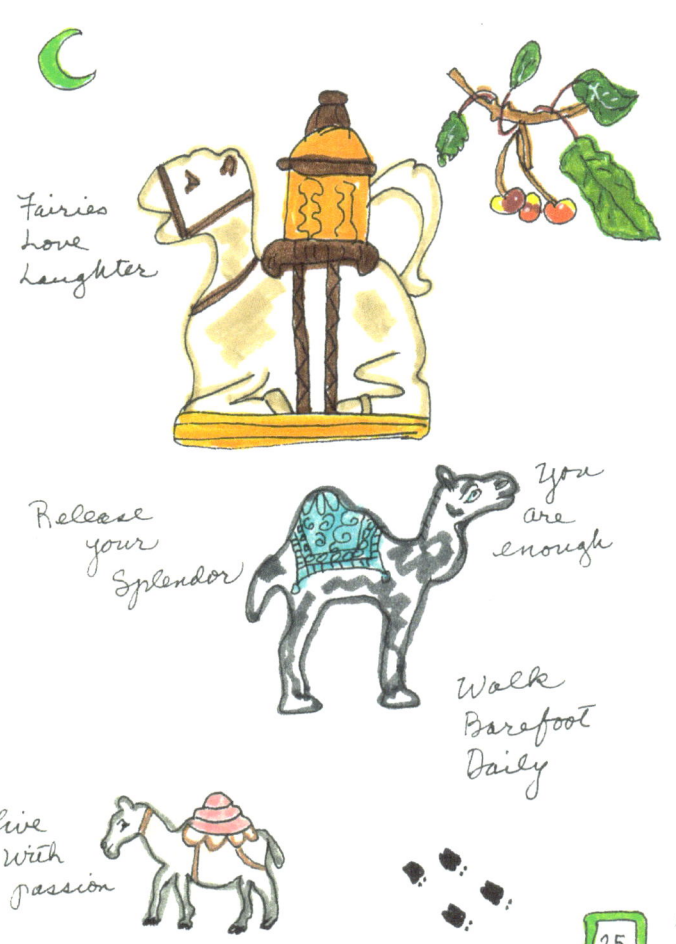

Fairies
Love
Laughter

Release
your
Splendor

You
are
enough

Walk
Barefoot
Daily

Live
with
passion

25.

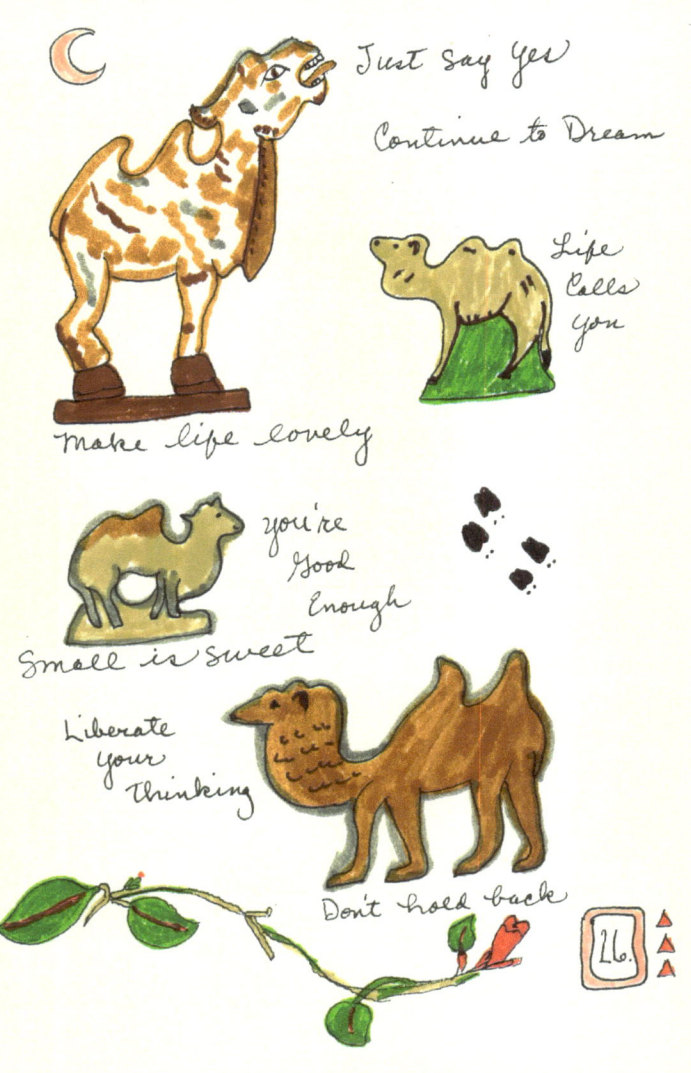

Just say Yes

Continue to Dream

Life
Calls
you

make life lovely

you're
Good
Enough

Small is sweet

Liberate
your
Thinking

Don't hold back

26.

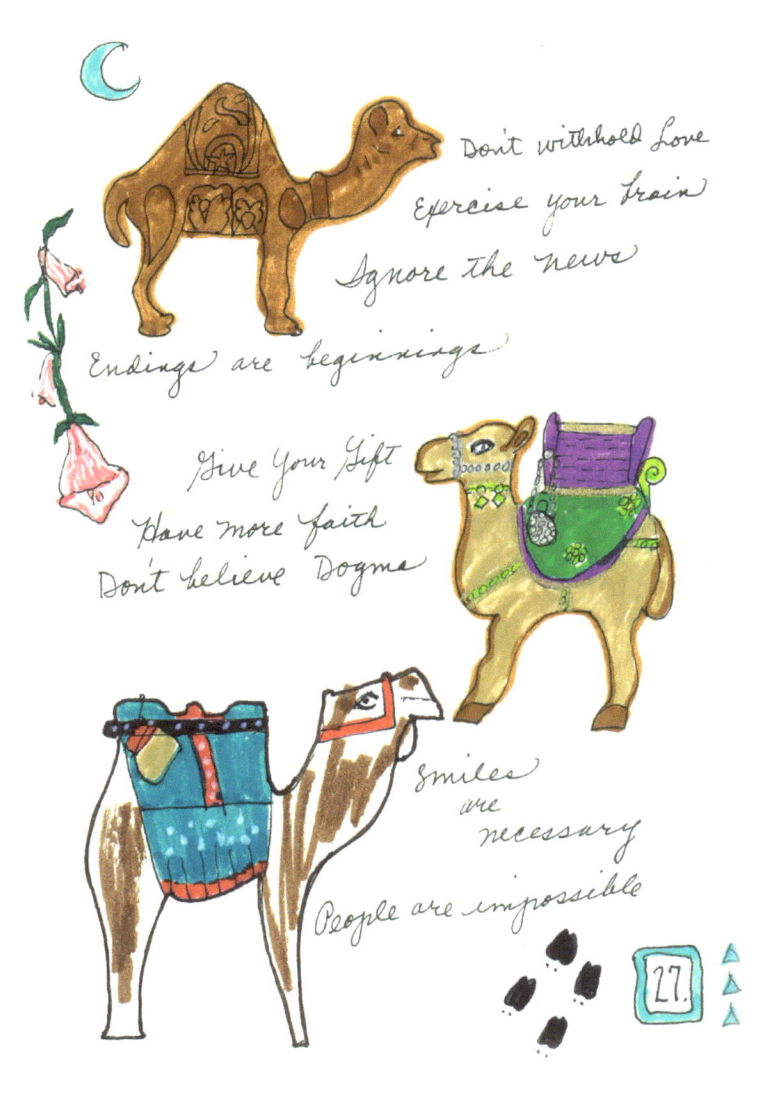

Don't withhold Love
Exercise your brain
Ignore the news

Endings are beginnings

Give Your Gift
Have more faith
Don't believe Dogma

Smiles
are
necessary

People are impossible

27.

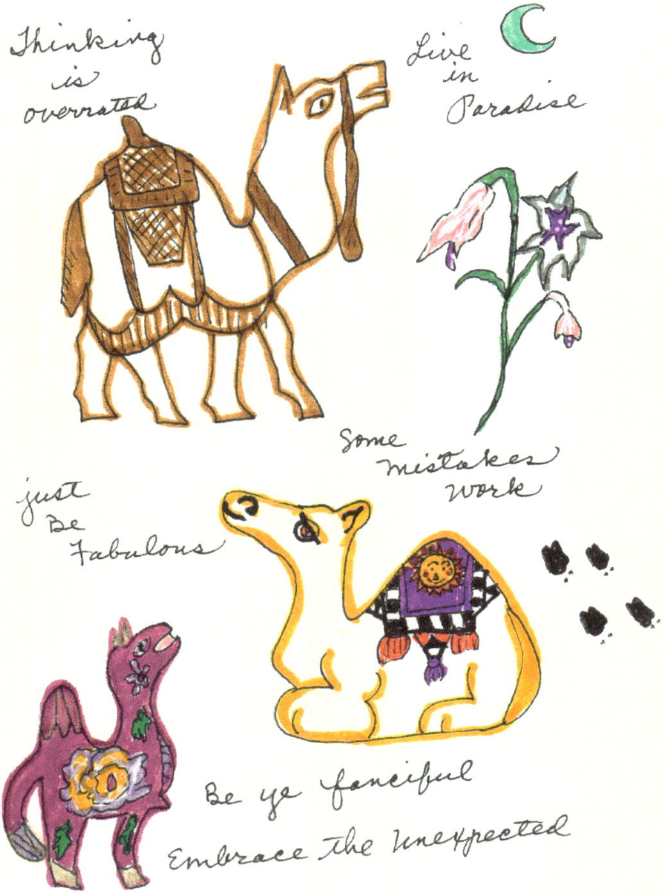

Thinking
is
overrated

Live
in
Paradise

Some
mistakes
work

just
Be
Fabulous

Be ye fanciful

Embrace the Unexpected

28.

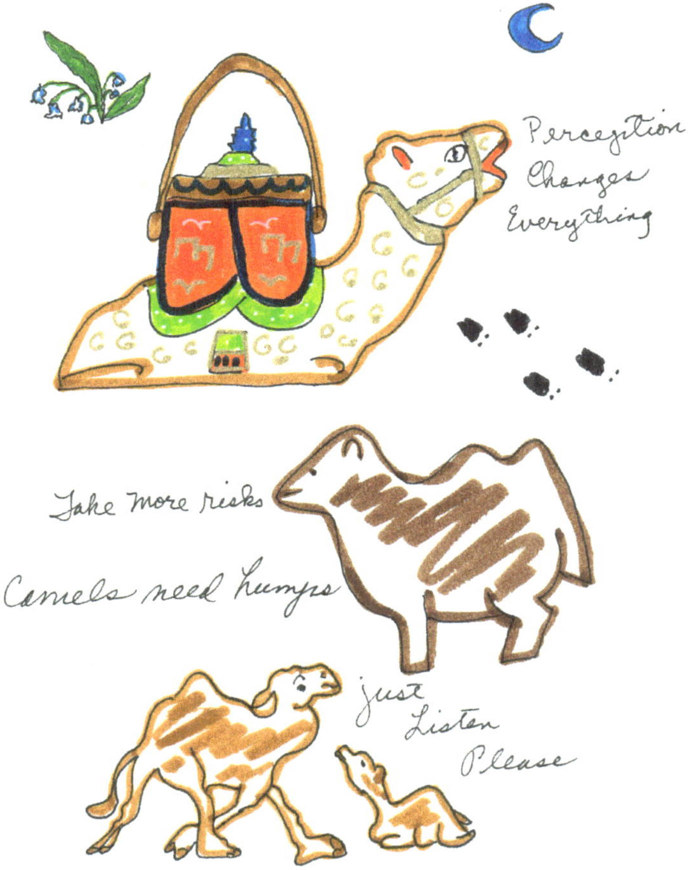

Perception
Changes
Everything

Take more risks

Camels need humps

Just
Listen
Please

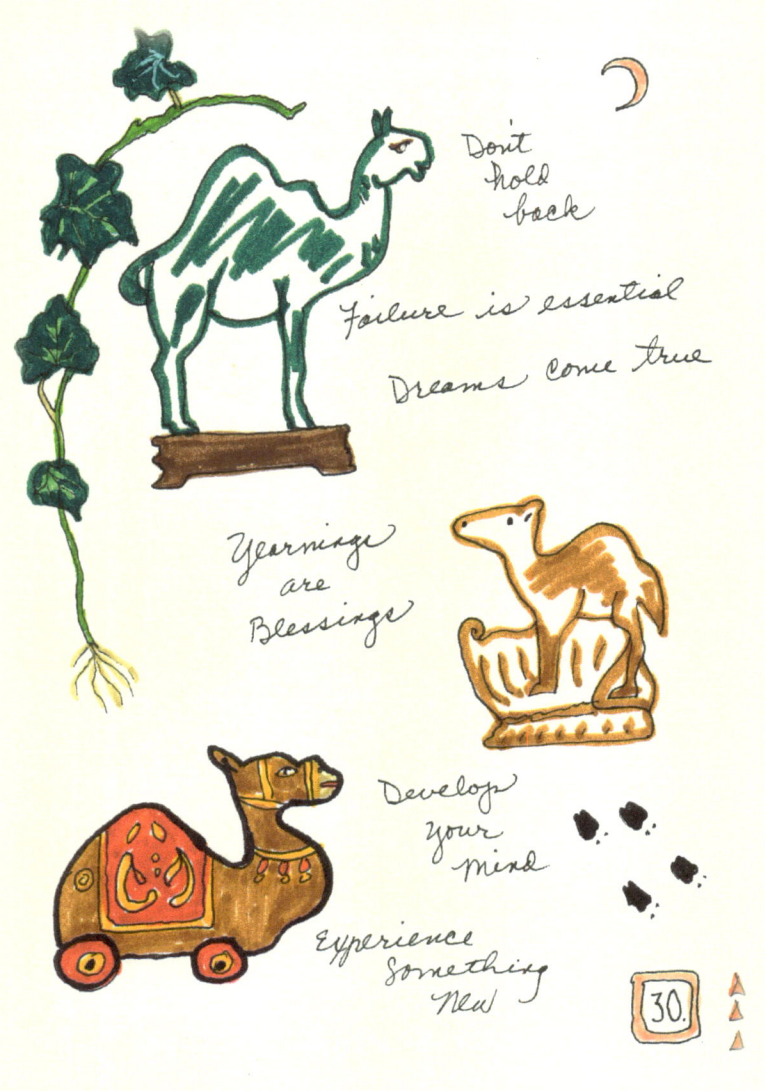

Don't
hold
back

Failure is essential

Dreams come true

Yearnings
are
Blessings

Develop
your
mind

Experience
Something
New

30.

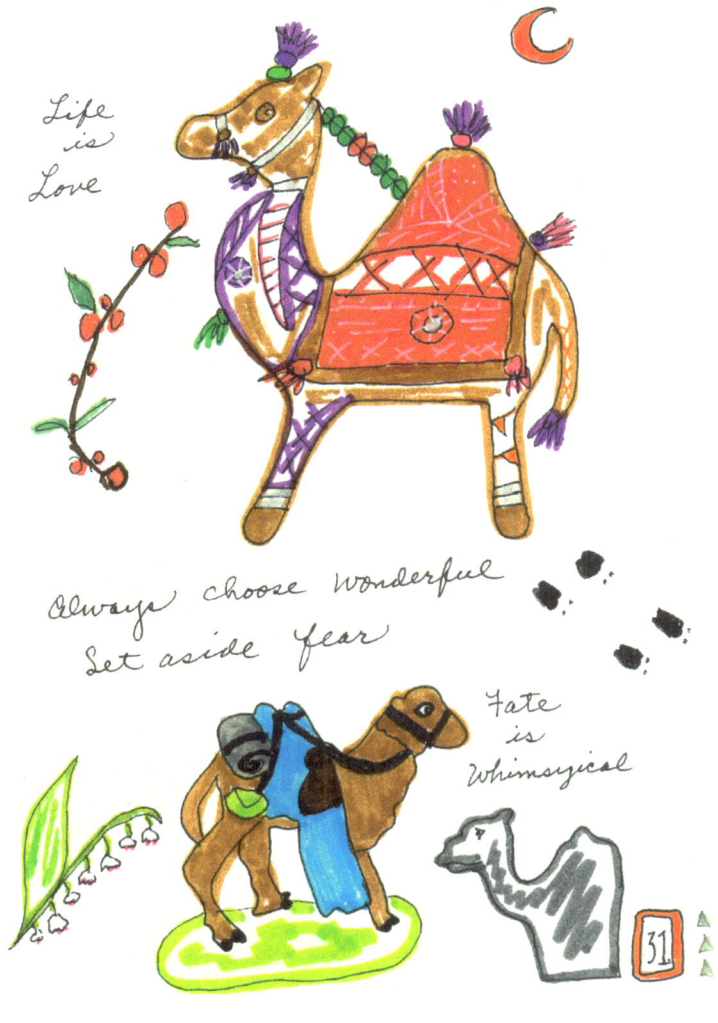

Life
is
Love

Always choose wonderful
Set aside fear

Fate
is
Whimsical

31

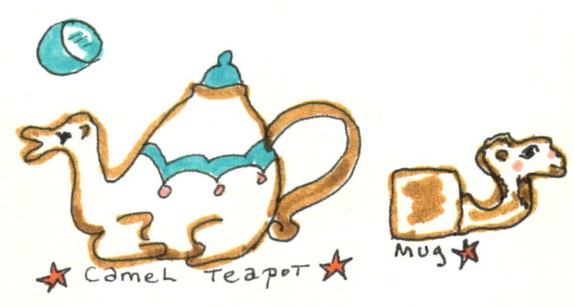

★ Camel Teapot ★   Mug ★

I have over 100 unique,
funny and beautiful camels,
a collection that started
when I was a child.
    I have used Camels for
centerpieces for Wedding
tables and other special
events.
    Each Camel shares a piece
of my heart and I love the
generous giver. I hope you
enjoy their words.
    I am Camel blessed!
        February 2014
        joann d. rosi

www.ingramcontent.com/pod-product-compliance
Lightning Source LLC
Chambersburg PA
CBHW041242200526
45159CB00030B/3022